Pebble
T0080616

Hea

Snacks for Healthy Teeth

by Mari Schuh

Consulting Editor:
Gail Saunders-Smith, PhD

Consultant:
Lori Gagliardi CDA, RDA, RDH, EdD

Capstone press®
Mankato, Minnesota

Pebble Plus is published by Capstone Press,
1710 Roe Crest Drive, North Mankato, Minnesota 56003.
www.capstonepub.com

Copyright © 2008 by Capstone Press, a Capstone imprint.
All rights reserved. No part of this publication may be reproduced in whole
or in part, or stored in a retrieval system, or transmitted in any form or by any means, electronic, mechanical,
photocopying, recording, or otherwise, without written permission of the publisher.
For information regarding permission, write to Capstone Press,
1710 Roe Crest Drive, North Mankato, Minnesota 56003.

Library of Congress Cataloging-in-Publication Data
Schuh, Mari C., 1975–
Snacks for healthy teeth/by Mari Schuh.
p. cm. — (Pebble plus. Healthy teeth)
Summary: "Simple text, photographs, and diagrams present information about healthy snacks for teeth and includes how to take care of teeth properly" — Provided by publisher.
Includes bibliographical references and index.
ISBN-13: 978-1-4296-1239-5 (hardcover)
ISBN-10: 1-4296-1239-8 (hardcover)
ISBN-13: 978-1-4296-1785-7 (softcover)
ISBN-10: 1-4296-1785-3 (softcover)
1. Nutrition and dental health — Juvenile literature. I. Title. II. Series.
RK281.S29 2008
617.6′01 — dc22 2007027116

Editorial Credits
Sarah L. Schuette, editor; Veronica Bianchini, designer and illustrator

Photo Credits
Capstone Press/Karon Dubke, all

The author dedicates this book to her husband, Joseph Quam.

Note to Parents and Teachers

The Healthy Teeth set supports national science standards related to personal health. This book describes and illustrates healthy snacks for dental health. The images support early readers in understanding the text. The repetition of words and phrases helps early readers learn new words. This book also introduces early readers to subject-specific vocabulary words, which are defined in the Glossary section. Early readers may need assistance to read some words and to use the Table of Contents, Glossary, Read More, Internet Sites, and Index sections of the book.

Printed in the United States 5725

Table of Contents

Good Snacks 4
Sweets 14
Healthy Teeth 18

Glossary 22
Read More 23
Internet Sites 23
Index 24

Good Snacks

Teresa eats good snacks.
They keep her teeth
and gums healthy
and strong.

Teresa eats vegetables
that are full of vitamins.
Vitamins help her body fight
diseases, even in her mouth.

Teresa's mouth makes
more saliva when
she eats fresh fruit.
Saliva washes away sugar
that causes decay.

Teresa likes milk, cheese,
and yogurt.
These foods have calcium.
Calcium makes teeth strong.

Teresa snacks on popcorn.
It doesn't stick to her teeth
like gooey sweets.

Old

Sweets

Sweets like candy and soda
can hurt the enamel
that protects your teeth.

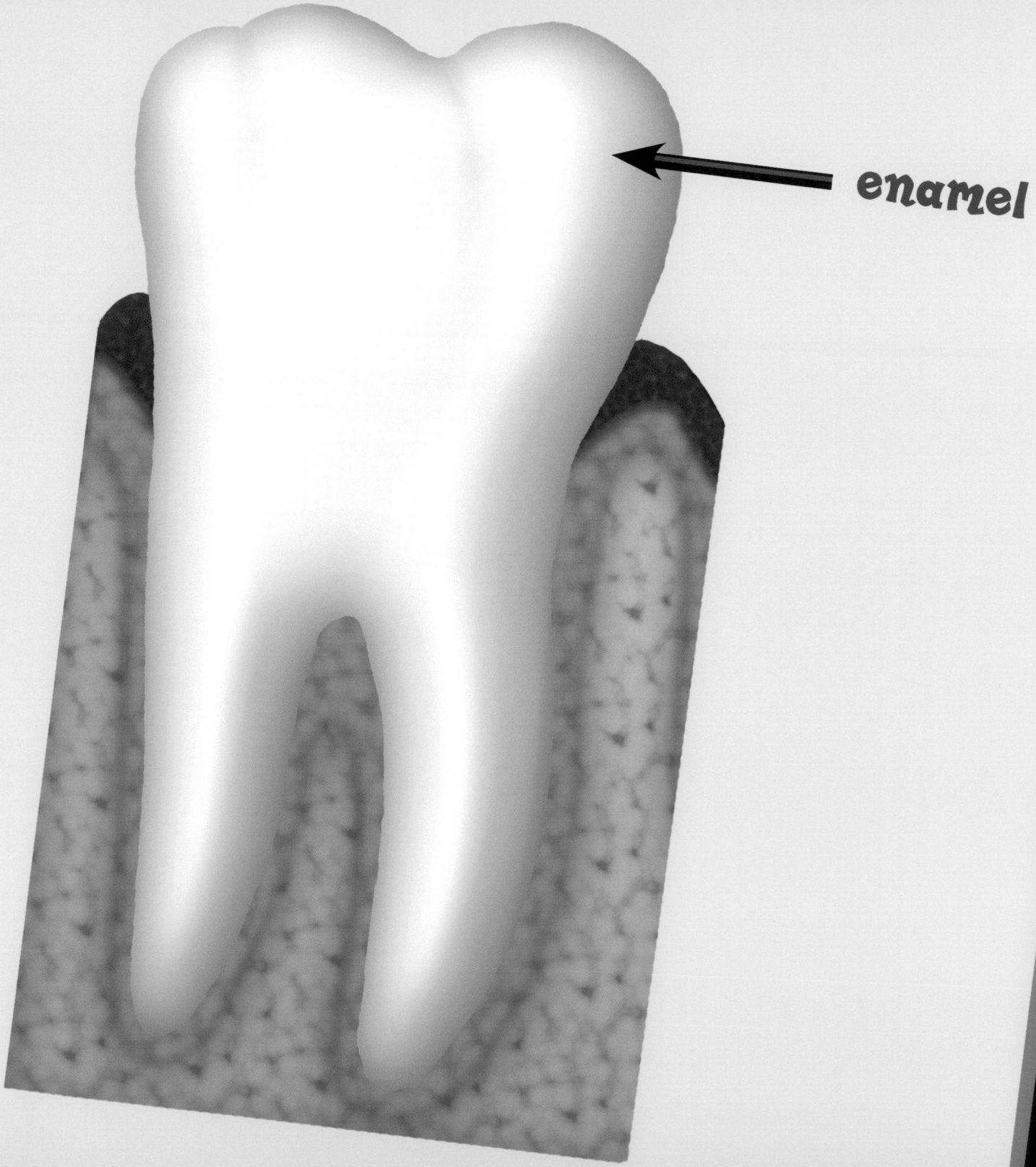
enamel

Germs in your mouth
turn sugar into acid.
Acid wears away enamel.
Acid causes decay
and cavities.

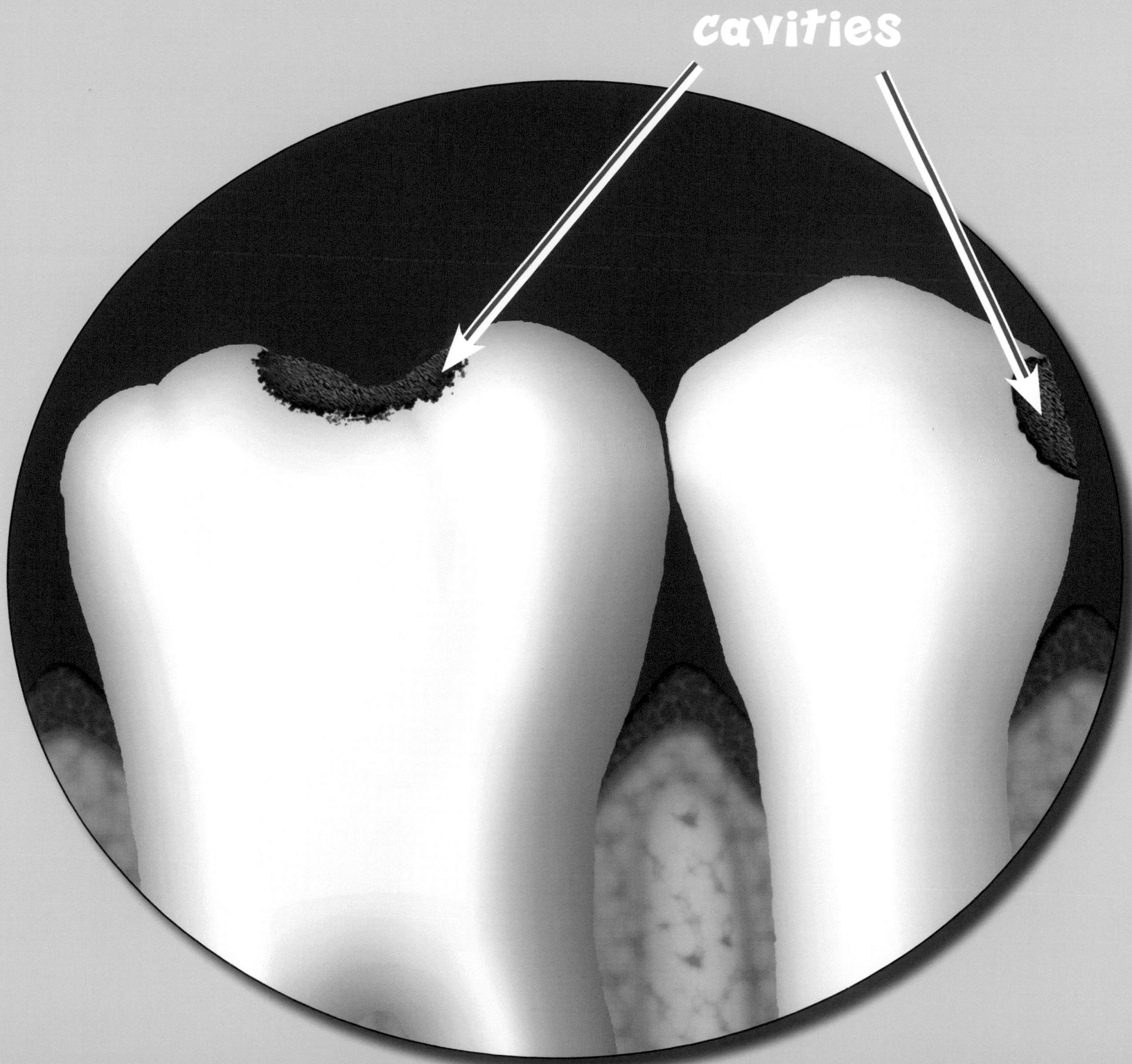
cavities

Healthy Teeth

Teresa brushes her teeth
to get rid of the acid.
Even rinsing
with water helps.

Follow Teresa's good example
and eat good snacks.
You'll have strong, healthy
teeth your whole life.

Glossary

acid — a liquid that wears away teeth; acid forms from germs and sugar in your mouth.

cavity — a decayed or broken-down part of a tooth; eating healthy snacks helps prevent cavities.

decay — to rot, break down, or make a hole in something

enamel — the hard, glossy covering on teeth; enamel protects teeth from decay.

gum — the firm skin around the base of teeth

saliva — the clear liquid in your mouth that keeps it moist, helps you swallow, and digest food

sweets — foods that have lots of sugar; candy, soft drinks, and cookies are sweets.

vitamin — a part of food that keeps you strong and helps protect you from getting sick

Read More

Kalman, Bobbie. *Super Snacks.* Kid Power. New York: Crabtree, 2003.

Royston, Angela. *Tooth Decay.* It's Not Catching. Chicago: Heinemann, 2004.

Schuh, Mari C. *Healthy Snacks.* Healthy Eating with MyPyramid. Mankato, Minn.: Pebble Books, 2006.

Internet Sites

FactHound offers a safe, fun way to find Internet sites related to this book. All of the sites on FactHound have been researched by our staff.

Here's how:

1. Visit *www.facthound.com*
2. Choose your grade level.
3. Type in this book ID **1429612398** for age-appropriate sites. You may also browse subjects by clicking on letters, or by clicking on pictures and words.
4. Click on the **Fetch It** button.

FactHound will fetch the best sites for you!

Index

acid, 16, 18
brushing, 18
calcium, 10
cavities, 16
cheese, 10
decay, 8, 16
diseases, 6
enamel, 14, 16
fruit, 8
germs, 16
gums, 4
milk, 10
popcorn, 12
rinsing, 18
saliva, 8
sugar, 8, 16
sweets, 12, 14
vegetables, 6
vitamins, 6
yogurt, 10

Word Count: 136
Grade: 1
Early-Intervention Level: 20